www.finishinglinepress.com

Cottonwood Strong
Bent but Not Broken

poems by

Lin Marshall Brummels

Finishing Line Press
Georgetown, Kentucky

Cottonwood Strong
Bent but Not Broken

ACKNOWLEDGMENTS

"Emerging" and "Letter to My 16-year-old Self Fifty Years Later" were
published in *Celebrate: A Collection of Writings by and about Women*, 2015.

Publisher: Leah Maines
Editor: Christen Kincaid
Cover Art: Lin Marshall Brummels
Author Photo: Elizabeth Brummels Daehnke
Cover Design: Leah Huete

Printed in the USA on acid-free paper.
Order online: www.finishinglinepress.com
        also available on amazon.com

Author inquiries and mail orders:
Finishing Line Press
P. O. Box 1626
Georgetown, Kentucky 40324
U. S. A.

Table of Contents

Introduction

I imagine my family tree twisting and turning like a Lowcountry Live Oak, but, it more resembles an old cottonwood that has survived the hard winters and strong winds of the Plains. The tree grew deep roots, dropped occasional branches, but continues to stand tall and offer shade on hot summer days.

I was raised by post-World War II parents who farmed with horses the first year or two after the war. My folks grew up during the Great Depression, and their parents were turn-of-the century farmers. All of them were financially strapped Nebraskans who kept their thoughts to themselves. My children are Nebraska's future.

I was a teenager during the "Summer of Love," the 1968 Chicago convention riots, and the growing women's movement. I believed life was happening in cities and on the coasts. I longed to live a different kind of life away from the farm, but was too young to leave home.

I was the first in my family to attend college during the last years of the Viet Nam War. I got married during my freshman year in college. My husband had a low draft number and a student deferment. He avoided the war because peace was declared the summer we graduated. We loaded our belongings into a Ryder truck and moved to upstate New York where he planned to attend graduate school at Syracuse University.

My first job after college was as a group home manager in Syracuse, N.Y. caring for adolescent boys. Many of them lived their entire lives in institutions before moving into this group home. These boys were part of the first group of disabled students to attend regular classes and participate in extracurricular activities with public school students. I took university classes to learn more about helping these youngsters during the years in the group home and along the way, earned a master's degree from Syracuse University.

This book of poems speaks to the idea of family; some who I count as blood relatives, and some as family imagined. Some I've' nurtured, some have encouraged me, some have been roadblocks, and some have passed on. Over the years, there have been hints of past abuse in my family of origin, but it was never directly acknowledged by perpetrators or victims.

One or more of the group home boys had been sexually abused and had resulting behavior problems. As I learned about how to help them, I learned to better understand my own story. These poems reflect my growing awareness of our family's issues, and my personal journey of survival.

HARLEY'S LEGACY

"Destruction Cometh; and they shall seek peace, and there shall be none."
Ezekiel 7.25

Granddaddy took the twins to the barn
when they were naughty.
Grandmamma didn't like to spank,
neither did he, or so he said.
He just tickled them,
made them laugh,
inspired them to tell their momma
they were sorry.

That's the legend but I believe
there's a back-story,
a tale of unsaid groping
and touching behind barn doors,
a saga of denial
closing that mother's eyes.

TWINS

Our twin mothers didn't look or act alike
but were each half of a whole
like a grapefruit split for breakfast,
my aunt kind and sweet, covered in sugar,
mom, acidic with pre-cut sections salted.

I was a bit saltier like my mama, my cousin
sugary like hers. We were only girls among
seven brothers. I wanted to be pretty like her.
We were sisters in our hearts, hiked the hills
and valleys near her home and dreamed.

She moved after high school
and we lost track. Mom said my cousin
became a model, hoped the same for me.

My aunt kept house for a doctor,
raised his nine kids after her own
until Auntie's breast cancer diagnosis
forced early retirement. Mother's
better angel died when she lost her twin;
twenty years later a tumor took Mom too.

I learned my cousin was a model-secretary;
Mom had only heard part of the story,
created her own conclusion, as was her way.

My cousin, raised old school, quit work
when she married, reconnected now
after thirty years, we're Facebook friends,
exchange Christmas cards,
today's version of walking the hills.

DOORWAYS WITHOUT DOORS

We move to a house of doorways,
tiny rooms with multiple openings,
wall-to-wall furniture,
illusions of privacy but everyone
knows everyone's business.

Little cracker-barrel house
doesn't have a plan, its rooms
stuck here or there like it was built
by drunk uncle Larry
three quarts into a day.

Porch full of coats, overshoes, stove cobs
welcomes visitors. In summer it smells
of moldy newspapers and freshly picked
veggies. The kitchen has the only indoor
plumbing. We do our daily business

out back in the outhouse. Cob-burner's
stove pipe angles over a tiny range,
water heater huddles in a corner,
table and chairs squeeze between
an old pantry and utility room.

Family gathers winter days,
watches the only channel on TV.
Oil burned warms its corner
and I escape to my chilly bedroom
to read and dream.

My room juts from the house's east end
like an-out-of-place Lego,
outside exit with a private porch
and a door that shuts,
away from brothers and all mine.

BACK HOUSE

Behind the house
facing east
toward the creek,
paint long gone,
door warped open
by summer rains
and winter snow,
stands the back house.

I learn to close my nose
as I near the two-holer,
concentrate
on deer grazing below
in the misty meadow
by the winding creek,
listen to birds sing
in near-by trees.

In winter, I wait
for my dad
to make his morning visit,
newspaper in hand
to melt frost,
snow and cold
from the big hole;
no one uses the little hole.

Family contributions
build unevenly;
next summer,
time to move the building.

CHILD

With a nod to the Little Match Girl and other children's stories

I Will Love You Forever
Where the Wild Ones Are.
The Little Match Girl
taught me the outside world
is just a shell
and even when
it is *bitterly cold outside,*
inner life alone matters,
beauty is not easily visible
or appreciated by others.
We can
still imagine eating roast duck,
or *Green Eggs and Ham*
at *Watership Down*
on elegant bone china
laid on a white clothed table
beneath a candle-lit Christmas tree.

LILLIE

Two four-year old girls turn toward the sound
of one anxious mother calling them,
fretful of dangers on the old tire swing.

Dark and light faces frame the weathered rubber,
shinning black and blond tresses glint red in the sun
merging them into one profile.

The petite country blond squints
 into afternoon's golden slant of light
 to see who calls to share her toy.

Urban born Lillie discovers rural fun
in the worn greying rustic swing,
her young hostess steps aside for Lillie's ride.

AMIR

Little friend already serious
in your blue jeans, striped shirt,
sporting a Harry Potter haircut
before Daniel Radcliff was born.

There on the bench with your sister
and my little daughter
east met west on my deck
without animosity or politics.

I lost track of you
since your family left
and now see you nearly every day
in the news prominently displayed

as a spy imprisoned without charge.
It leaves my heart upside down
and crying for your sweet parents
lost in a world of worry.

GET ME THEM LIPS

Twelve-year-old Willie
smiles a big-ass grin
visible in the mirror
propped on the table.
I watch
him repeatedly comb
through my hair,
feel the teeth gently
bounce over my skull
as the comb moves
through my long brown locks.
He stands behind my chair,
says in his best Bronx falsetto,
"I'm gonna get me them lips,"
pretends to steal a kiss
while he brushes, combs
and grins.

LEARNING TO RIDE

I inherited a 26-inch bike with a hard seat
from brothers who rode gravel roads with ease
and took turns laughing and teasing
until I forked the middle bar in the July heat,
found coasting downhill quite a treat.
I picked up speed in a warm south breeze
then hit gravel in the shade of some trees
and the front wheel turned in a heartbeat.

I tried to use my toes to stop the spin
of the bike before it fell, but slid off the seat,
got it tangled in my feet and fell in the road,
hit my head, skinned knees and shins,
then shook it off determined to avoid defeat,
pushed off again balancing my weight's load.

WINDMILL BOUND

Chip was a distant cousin,
son of Mom's cousin's daughter;
same age as us, real first cousins.

His family only attended
clan gatherings on Mom's
and her twin sister's birthday.

After dinner at my cousin's farm
we went outside for girl talk
behind the barn.

Chip sneaked around the corner,
chased us across the barnyard,
toward the windmill,

threatened to tell our parents
everything he thought he heard,
laughed at our worry.

We made a plan,
led the chase around the shed,
grabbed some rope,

tied one end to the windmill tower,
waited for him to catch us.
We wrapped the rope around

and around Chip,
bound him to the tower,
tied the other end to a post,

walked casually back to the house,
just in time to sing "Happy Birthday,"
eat ice cream and cake.

WHISKEY

"None of you shall approach to any that is near of kin to him, to uncover their nakedness: I am the Lord."
Leviticus 19.6

My cousin and I are three months apart,
grow up together, trade sleep-overs
every summer. She, the youngest
with two older sisters and a brother
my older brother's age.
I'm a middle kid with younger
brothers, too, always underfoot.
It's special to step into her world of girls.

My parents' tiny house offers
little room for privacy and girl talk.
Her family home is spacious,
rooms rambling but disconnected.
My aunt and uncle inattentive,
leave us free to wander in and out
all day or late into the night.

We roam pastures by moonlight,
whisper secrets about boys
and our dreams, share a pint jar
of bad whiskey from her dad's bottle.
"He'll never miss this," she assures me,
a worrier at thirteen.

White Label or Old Grandfather,
or something worse didn't matter,
it's an introduction to a grown up
world. Whiskey burns my throat
the first drink, then warms a spot
in my belly I didn't know existed,
lowers my reserve. We share
family secrets.

NERVES

No time after school to eat
        bus home
        milk cows
        back to town

October football see-your-breath night
        my hands in ice water
        grab bottles of cold coke
        to sell to excited fans
        during game with rival team

My turn to help clean field after game
        Few use trash cans
        We pick up crumpled popcorn sacks
        candy bar wrappers
        empty bottles left behind

Date after game with cool lineman
        can't catch my breath
        light headed and dizzy
        Date ruined
        he takes me home

Parents worry
        brother drives car to hospital
        Dad sits with me in back
        shows concern usually hidden
        behind his gruff face

Neligh Memorial admits me at midnight
        Good night's sleep
        no morning chores
        breakfast in bed

Nerves the doctor says
        Discharge by noon

EMERGING

I learned early about evil
when he poked sticks at me
on my tricycle
when I was three,
paid me pennies at six to undress,
came to my bed when I was eight,
peaked in bathroom windows
to see me naked at ten.

Overly sensitive
according to my family,
felt slights when none
were intended,
heard insults
when nothing happened,

but they didn't know
or turned a blind eye
to my menacing brother.
I saw him shove his brothers,
break windows.

I felt constant dread,
wonder who I might have been
but for changed wiring in my brain;
a life-long legacy
of avoiding conflicts,
hiding from raised voices
and physical struggle.

Skeptical of others' motives,
I listen carefully to spot tricks,
eventually devising a means
of measuring bullshit by peering
into peoples' eyes to see
if they have a soul.

READY TO BELIEVE

He was lab supervisor
during my first college job,
wore beautifully tailored jackets,
spoke with a British accent
matching his dark skin.

He told me I was beautiful,
wasted on local hicks,
painted pictures of life
in the exotic land of his birth,
invited me for tea, gave
me a sari I couldn't accept.

I realized his agenda too late,
*what did you expect
when you came to my home?*

I didn't know about grooming,
nor understand it was rape
until years later,
longed to tell my love,
afraid he'd blame me too.

SHADOWS

The yellow Porsche follows me
as I walk to and from class every day,
reminding me

his bed nestles in a windowed alcove,
bright even with the shades drawn,
bed covers tossed aside. He doesn't

look at me, dresses, leaves the room.
He hits a ball through a window.
I say, "Knock on their door and offer

to pay the damages."
He pretends not to hear,
walks away.

"I'm sorry but your name disappeared
from the electronic calendar,
the schedule is booked with others."

I say, "You can't treat this student
one way and another differently,"
but no one listens.

I begin to run from shadows,
hide in alleys and behind bushes,
afraid of being found again

by the man in the yellow car. My inner
voice screams, but I must be invisible.
No one hears my pleas.

MIDDLE GROUND

This country place was to be middle ground
between a city-loft and summer-cabin,
living rural near a means of making a living.
I was happy walking to work in my adopted town,
now I go to great lengths to be where I can't be found.
Our union should have allowed us to be more giving,
and work as a unit respecting each other's opinion
but it's too much life to see around.

Our children arrive in their own good time,
tiny bundles of joy wrapped in piles of diapers.
Busy jobs in town, children's school events,
time with friends keep us too busy to get out of line.
Kids in college and our daughter's trip to the altar
leave us with an empty nest and discontent.

ALWAYS THE CONTRAST

Just the two children to launch,
oldest left home with his buds,
preferring to make his own way,
youngest daughter wanted me there
every step of her journey.
I had her home for a few more years
and when she left I cried for days.

My husband hefted a glass or three
with his buddies, our shared goals done.
He didn't want to travel with me,
I didn't want to bar hop,
flew to Portugal with my friends.
He rode horseback with his, across the plains
and we never quite came together again.

LETTER TO MY SIXTEEN-YEAR-OLD SELF FIFTY YEARS LATER

Hey kid, be patient, don't run away,
you'll be old enough to leave home
soon; finish high school,
figure out your future.

Don't fool yourself, you're too young
to run away. You don't have a clue
how to take care of yourself, never
held a job, not even volunteer work.

Bury your head in books, try to be polite
to your family. They're doing as well
as possible given their limited income,
post WW II attitudes.

Talk to your dad. He is a thoughtful
man, but doesn't know how to communicate
with his wife and daughter. He does fine
chatting with his sons or other men.

Don't be intimidated when your mother
threatens "wait till your father gets home".
Try to understand Dad doesn't want to deal
with ornery kids after long days in the field.

Caution your brother to let go of mulishness
like refusing to pass the pepper to Dad
when he's hungry; step up and protect
him from resulting blows.

Hey kid, speak up for yourself, be obnoxious
occasionally; don't go through life silently
angry at your Mom for not protecting her children,
guilty when Dad's anger passes you, visits a brother.

DAD LOVES THE RITUAL

Milking cows with octopus machines
attached to their teats, buckets hanging
from straps around the cows' flanks
is a bit of an art even on good days.

Dad stops in the middle of darn-near anything,
even milking,
to roll a cigarette
with tobacco from a Velvet can,
carefully opening the lid,
arranging the inner lining
to serve as a spout with one hand
while sliding a Zig-Zag paper
from the packet,
cupping it into a half-circle,
holding it in place with the other
all the while tapping
a little tobacco across the paper,
closing the Velvet lid,
sliding the can back into his pocket,
holding the paper quite still
than bringing both hands to bear
on the task of rolling,
licking the last edge to seal the sides,
twisting each end
bringing it to his lips with one hand
while the other searches another pocket
for a kitchen match
and in one continuous process
pulls the match rapidly across his jeans
from knee to thigh to light every time,
raises the match to the twisted end
while cupping that hand around the flame
protecting against any sudden breezes,
insuring a lit smoke time and again.

Suction cups let go,
suck dusty air, the mama moos,
device dangles between her feet,
but he doesn't move until he finishes this ritual
and inhales.

LOST IN THE EIGHTIES

After college in the early eighties
my baby brother joined the Army,
believed in the military like his big brother
before him, met a pretty girl in class,
married her on a frigid winter day.

They followed his career together
as couples did then. He was lost
when she left him for a woman.
It was early days for gay pride,
broke his farm-boy heart.

He cried during calls to me, calls he couldn't
make to our folks, finally told them
she'd left him. I wanted to believe he felt better
when time stretched between calls and talk
turned to the weather.

Promoted out of a downsized military
he became another unemployed veteran,
tried to sell a house no one wanted
when the economy tanked, moved
seeking work and settled in Aberdeen.

He sold his Carolina house at a loss,
finally saved for another down-payment
on a new place in a good neighborhood,
in a new city, proudly talked about his new
home, new job, adopted shelter dog.

Keeping a façade of respectability,
he grew flowers, walked his dog, met a woman
walking her dog and moved her into his house.
He paid for other women on the sly, maxed
his credit cards, borrowed against his home and cars.

A double life, weight gain, and lies mixed
into a toxic cocktail. Aneurism and stroke
left him brain-dead at fifty-three. His live-in lady
couldn't make decisions about his care, called
my brothers and me to decide if he lived or died.

OBSESSIONS

My world works best
when all the pieces
are in place,

windows sparkling in the sun,
furniture in harmony
with an unspoken order,

boxelder bugs and spiders
stay outside or enjoy
short lives,

lights are bright enough
for my poor eyes to read
small print,

night is dark enough
to see the Milky Way
stretch across the sky,

mice stay out of the
house or eat poison
and die,

cats don't shed
much or scratch
the upholstery,

dog chases pests
away from the house,
sleeps by the fire.

ASTONISHMENT

Bent forward as far as possible
over my bulging nine-month belly,
the long needle enters near my spine.
My legs are numb first, then hips,
pain receptors muted south of my waist,
hands wheel me to a sterile stage

peopled with masked players.
A needle-wielder sits by my head,
talks in soothing tones.
Two veiled actors pull drapes
across my stomach, shield my view
of scalpel, clamps, and gore.

Blades tickle my stretched skin.
A tug, then wrench as they pull
baby from her watery home.
"It's a girl" a narrator announces
behind the curtain, introducing
the leading lady.

Little bundle blanketed in pink
with reddish-black hair standing on end
salutes the afternoon.
She looks as astonished as I feel.
Her tiny hands refuse to stay covered.
Our wall phone rings after

she is home just a few days.
A stranger's voice summons
this babe for testing, confirms
a diagnosis, doctors already know
but want to eyeball the infant
and tell us face-to-face.

WHITE TEDDY BEAR

Stories in the news
describe a blonde, pretty, nine-year-old
left too much alone.

Her discarded t-shirt and jeans
discovered by hunters
near a wildlife refuge's watery terrain.

One of the suspects questioned
in the girl's disappearance
was never charged.

He moved into an old house
up the hill on this minimum-maintenance road
between us and the way out.

His interest in our daughter alarming.
At three, big blue eyes, blonde hair
she hides behind my knee.

A child-size white teddy bear
fills the sparsely furnished living room
in the old man's house.

He left in the night
as suddenly as he came,
broken furniture and toys left behind.

That old house up the hill
was burned for firemen's practice that year.
She may be buried there,

but no one checked for a little grave
concealed under the dirt basement floor
or in nearby corn fields.

JAZZ

The girls move in unison,
choreographed dancers
wearing matching dresses,

almost all in step,
high school sanitized version
of night club magic.

They don't know
Joel Grey knocked them dead
in real musicals

long before they were a twinkle
in their parents' eyes
or that Liza Minnelli wasn't famous

when cast for the movie
or that Cabaret changed
musical theatre.

They don't know that Nazis
were brutal war criminals
responsible for millions of deaths

not objects of fun
like Hogan's Heroes reruns
or even that the world struggled

to curb Nazi power.
They can't guess
that poets will

use words like music
to satirize it all years
after they go to college,

get married and raise
daughters who will someday
be part of swing choir.

MISSING

My daughter's baby book
headed for higher ground
in the downpour, last week.

It didn't tell me where it went
to find shelter from the rain.
Lawnmower's gas can

took a hike from its customary
spot in the shed. It didn't like
the wheel barrow's company

since he started to swear
and rant about politics.
The garden spade protested

its duties tending brush fires
last winter, didn't want to devote
another spring to digging graves

for failed kittens,
left with no forwarding address.
I imagine the missing items

together under palm trees
on a tropical beach.
Shovel lounges beside gas can,

reads excerpts from
her baby book, uttering
an occasional ooh, ah.

LIFE'S GIFTS

Raised with four brothers,
work life surrounded by menfolk,
my first born a sweet baby boy,
I expected only fellas in my world.

It was a thing of wonder when doctors
pulled a baby girl from my womb.
I was thrilled to be gifted a female
by Mother Nature.

My son announced his engagement
with a single texted word "engaged"
after thirty-three years of decided singleness
and the family gained another beautiful lass.

Waking every day in good health,
rising before sunrise to write,
hours are gifts, entire days precious,
weeks and months are grace extended.

WEDDING PLANNING

A winter afternoon at sunset,
we ford snow-melt rivers,
skirt standing pools,
tromp through slushy drifts,
lingering in shadows,
after days of thawing,
to climb Lone-Pine Hill.

The Mother of the bride and I inspect
the proposed wedding location
on this wind-swept snowy knoll,
imagine the scene in summer
filled with laughing guests,
engaged couple trading vows
under an August sky at sunset.

We discuss catering, flowers,
getting new dresses,
practical shoes,
transporting the elderly Grandmothers
and those unable to hike this hill,
parking for guests,
and the chances of rain in August.

BACHELOR PARTY

Zeke walks across the Sandhills
the weekend before his wedding.
Dakota and Griff share the hike
to celebrate the upcoming marriage.

They enjoy sunrise and set
unhindered by buildings, trees, or people,
crisp mornings on hot airless days,
skinny dipping in cattle tanks.

On the trip home, his back
and right buttock turn bright red,
blister, itch like hell. Dakota
believes Zeke shat in poison ivy.

He returns to six days of wedding prep,
unable to sit for long, walking hurt,
blisters grow as temps rise past ninety
every day all week.

Cleaning buildings, raising tent,
moving tables, and chairs enflame his flesh
covered with calamine lotion
from collarbone to butt-crack.

Cold showers, salve, steroids
allows him to sit a saddle,
gallop his mare across grassland
to meet his bride for a sunset ceremony.

MOMMA

On Mother's Day afternoon
after a city backyard brunch
we drive to the south pasture
to check the cattle water.

Cows and calves are thirsty
this warm afternoon. As soon as
my son lifts the windmill brake,
its blades begin a slow spin
in a ten-mile-an-hour wind,
pumping water into the tank.

We glance up the mostly-grazed hill
to see a five-year-old cow move
away from the rest of the herd,
find a private place, hunch her back
to begin delivery.

A shiny Angus baby slides
from the birth canal of this three-time
momma with an ease
most mothers might envy.

We walk past a wetland choked
with cattails, up the hill to see
if the baby is born alive. Cow bends
her head, licks afterbirth, naturally
as chewing her cud.

Calf lies where it fell,
then lifts its head,
stretches long legs.

REMEMBER NOVEMBER

Moving from daylight savings
to so-called regular time
on Guy Fawkes Day without
changing work hours
blows up routines.
My body clock doesn't
adjust as easily as
the timepieces that run life.

Although loss of light
is gradual in Autumn,
one day I drive
twelve miles into a brilliant
morning sun and return to hours
of bright evenings, and the next day
my trip to town is in the dark
and the return voyage
is into murky dusk.

Remember, time can't
be changed like a runner
discards dirty socks.
Recall the Fifth of November's
failed attempt to overthrow
the crown with a celebration
of bonfires to light the night.

Lin Marshall Brummels grew up on a farm near the Nebraska Sandhills. She earned a bachelor's degree in Psychology from the University of Nebraska-Lincoln. Her first job after college was managing a group home for developmentally disabled adolescents in Syracuse, NY. She earned a master's degree from Syracuse University in Rehabilitation Counseling. After moving back to Nebraska, she became a Nebraska licensed mental health practitioner and certified professional counselor. She works as a private practice counselor. Brummels is a member of the Northern Lights Writing Group. She's the mother of two adult children, Zeke and Liz.

Brummels has published poetry in several journals, and her essay *Civilization* was published in *Ankle High and Knee Deep*, a collection of women's reflections on western rural life. Her poetry chapbook *Hard Times*, published by Finishing Line Press in 2015, won the 2016 Nebraska Book Award for chapbooks.

CPSIA information can be obtained
at www.ICGtesting.com
Printed in the USA
BVHW040309171021
619084BV00006B/137

9 781635 348415